MY DEAR DAUGHTER

Letters of Love, Life & Values

MY DEAR DAUGHTER

Letters of Love, Life & Values

April Zhou

Copyright ©2018 by April Zhou.

All rights reserved.

Published by Morgen Ventures LLC.

ISBN: 978-1-7324231-3-8
eBook ISBN: 978-1-7324231-6-9

Library of Congress Control Number: 2018946892

Cover background painted by Morgen Darnell
Edited by Stephen Darnell and Kiera Darnell
Printed in the U.S.A

www.aprilzhou.com

To my daughters,
Morgen & Kiera,
who are my inspirations for everything.

CONTENTS

One: Say Goodbye to Procrastination.....................3

Two: Focusing on the Positives.............................7

Three: The Beauty of a Small Bathroom 11

Four: Gymnastics, Math, and Others....................13

Five: Take a Risk; Take a Chance 17

Six: Bamboo, My Favorite Plant in the Whole Wide World 21

Seven: Free Hamilton Tickets? YES!!! 27

Eight: Starbucks Coffee I..31

Nine: Starbucks Coffee II 35

Ten: Whatever You Do, Give it Your All..............41

Eleven: Living for a Purpose 45

Twelve: Books Are Our Lifelong Friends.............49

Thirteen: The Schedule of Life...............................55

Fourteen: Kai Yuan Jie Liu（开源节流）, a Personal Wealth Secret..59

Fifteen: Snowballing Your Friends 65

Sixteen: 1,000 Kilometers in 2016 - What I Learned from Running 71

Seventeen: Fear is Best Conquered by Ability 83

Eighteen: First Things First....................................87

Nineteen: The World Was Wide Enough.............93

Twenty: Pay it Forward 97

Twenty-One: A Woman That You Grow Up to Become 101

Twenty-Two: My Desire to Share "My Dear Daughter" Entries 107

One

February 3rd, 2016

Say Goodbye to Procrastination

When I was going through one of the toughest periods of my life not so long ago, I kept asking myself what I would do if it were the last day of my life? The answer, I found out, would be to share with my daughters what I had experienced and learned. If so, why didn't I do it right away instead of waiting for the last day?

I set a goal for myself to write at least two "My Dear Daughter" letters each week in 2016. It is February 3rd today, and I am just starting. Why didn't I write something on January 1st, January 2nd, January 10th, January 20th, or February 1st? Was it because that I did not have anything to write about? No! I wanted to write about

Morgen's math challenges and our conversation about how everyone was good at different things, just like how different flowers and trees in the world were all pretty in their own ways. I wanted to write about how impressed I was with Morgen's investing philosophy. I wanted to write about Kiera's friendship discussion. I wanted to write about how striving for perfection and allowing yourself to make mistakes were equally important for Kiera. I wanted to write about how talented she was with languages. I wanted to write about what women should do in order to look and feel good after age 40 (I know that seems to be an eternity away to you now), and many other things....

So why on Earth did I not write anything in January? It was procrastination. I once lost one of my biggest teeth to procrastination. I ignored my doctor's advice and let my gum infection go on and worsen for two years. In the end, I had to get my tooth pulled because an abnormal substance grew so large, and the only way to clean it out completely was to remove the tooth. Now food gets stuck around the implanted tooth, and I have to floss after every meal or snack. Implants are great but they're never as effective as our own teeth because our gums do not grow tightly around them. Nobody told me in the past. I had to find that out the hard way. This is just one example of the price I have had to pay because of procrastination.

There are lots of other things I do not do promptly as well. It's almost like I have not suffered enough from procrastination because I keep doing it. I think I feel uncertain about results and the future so I wait to make decisions, to take action, and then wait some more. The truth is nobody can see into their future or guarantee positive results. People can analyze, plan, and anticipate, but they will only see results when they actually do something. What if the results are not what you desire? (That actually happens a lot, by the way). Make changes and try again until you are happy. Seriously, taking action is the most important and best thing you can do for yourself.

No procrastination.

It is the No. 1 most important thing that I have learned so far in life.

You both are special, talented, and have genius inside of you. I realize that you have your own opinions and might not completely agree with what I am saying in these "My Dear Daughter" letters. I am aware that raising children is also a process of educating and improving myself. I aim to become a better person every day. I hope you find that some of my words here are helpful.

Thank you for reading this and allowing me to share some of my thoughts with you.

I love you very much. - Mama

Two

May 2nd, 2016

Focusing on the Positives

Coming back from a lovely vacation in Florida, we discovered some of our house guest's belongings such as facial cleanser, moisturizer, a brow pencil, etc. in our upstairs bathroom. The one question we were all curious about is why he had an eyebrow pencil. Waking up the next morning to a gray raining sky, Kiera and I cuddled and talked. She said, "Walking into someone's private space like a bathroom, you can find out more about that person. What would he use the eyebrow pencil for?"

Kiera's comment reminded me of something that I once read from a book called *The Power of Habit: Why You Do What You Do In Life And Business*. The book pretty much says that walking into someone's apartment unannounced and having a look around for thirty minutes can let you really get to know the person. That is much more useful than, say, interacting or spending time with the individual a few times a week for several weeks or months. The reason for this is that we humans tend to show our best side in front of others. For example, we always try to straighten up our house before a guest visits, and we tend to talk about our happy experiences more often than sad ones.

I started to give examples of how a person's apartment could show his or her true personality and habits such as dirty clothes on the floor, a messy table, dirty dishes in the kitchen, and more. Kiera stopped me and said, "Why are you only focusing on the negative things?" She caught me; I was very negative. Instead of saying organized bookshelves, a color-coded closet, creatively decorated walls, or a labeled label-maker, I only had eyes for not-so-perfect areas.

What's the color of the world? If you ask a thousand people, you might get a thousand different answers. Blue, purple, pink, yellow, green, etc. The world is really what you perceive it to be. You are who you think you are. If you can see good things happening despite natural disasters, wars, corruption, etc., then the world is a beautiful place. Just like with Alice and Greta from the children's book *Alice and Greta: A Tale of Two Witches*, who lived on top of the same mountain and went to the same wizarding school, but because their perceptions were so different, they seemed to live in opposite worlds.

Girls, please accept my apology for seeing and talking too much about the negatives.

Lastly, I made it my goal to write to you two or three times every week because I have so much to share with you. In reality, I only wrote twice during the first four months. Looking back, I can't find any reason why I did not do what I planned on doing. I could beat myself up, but I will not. I will look at the positive side of this: I am restarting now.

You are the best. I love you very much. - Mama

Three

May 4th, 2016

The Beauty of a Small Bathroom

I love the fact that our family practically shares a small bathroom on the second floor. How small is it? There is just enough space for the entire family to stand in it at the same time. That's it.

Despite the small space, Morgen, Kiera and I sometimes would squeeze in at the same time - one using the sink; one taking a footbath, and one trimming nails in front of the window - even when we are not in a rush. Sure, we are all girls, so privacy may not be so much of an issue among us.

For some families, members don't like each other very much. They may even be enemies. For some families, members love each other but keep a distance. They can't be so physically close to each other. For other families, they love each other and feel happy together. We are one of the last type of families.

I am thankful for our small bathroom because it gives us an opportunity to learn to be together and stay close to each other. I am grateful that we are such a close family.

One day, we will complete our renovation and won't have to all squeeze into a small bathroom any more. I will miss our small bathroom. But I know that we will always be close to each other at heart.

I love you very much. - Mama

Four

May 23rd, 2016

Gymnastics, Math, and Others

Kiera honey, you seemed sad and disappointed after the NY State Gymnastics Championship. I was sad because you were. At the same time, I felt proud too because you achieved your best scores for the season. You learned and improved on your skills. You put in lots of effort and time. You had so many rips on your little hands. You overcame mental blocks and continued. And most of all, I was happy for you because I knew you had fun doing all these things and being a gymnast. You missed gymnastics so much during holiday breaks and couldn't wait to go back. You are a passionate gymnast! Next season, you will have more fun and become an even stronger gymnast mentally and physically. The kid who took first place this season might worry about losing. But you will have nothing to worry about but chasing your dream.

Congratulations on getting into the math 7 accelerated class! I know that it is what you wanted. You sounded so excited when you broke the news to me. Lots of your friends and kids you know got in too. It's a privilege. It must feel good to belong. You see, all these kids will grow up, go to different colleges, go into different professions, live their lives in their own ways. Some of them will become mathematicians; some of them singers; kids who love everything modern, like you, could become futurists. There are so many possibilities ahead. Naturally, in the end, some people feel more satisfied with their lives than others. No matter what the callings are, one will feel more satisfied and truly belonged when she discovers who she is and what she wants to spend her time on. Along the way, what she enjoys doing also helps people around her and makes the world a better place. Having and pursuing dreams make people whole.

You are required to learn about different subjects and things at school, whether you are interested in them or not. Honestly, I don't think that you have to excel in all subjects just because you want to have a perfect GPA. No one is good at everything. Instead, it would be more beneficial to spend time on things that you are interested in, figuring out how knowledge you acquire at school relates to the world and can be applied to benefit the world. Equally important is to explore interests outside of the school curriculum, to spend time on and develop a passion that will help you get to where you ultimately want to be.

I love you very much. - Mama

Five

May 25th, 2016

Take a Risk; Take a Chance

The other day, Kiera burst out "I took a risk today!" at the moment she got home. She could not wait to share what had happened at her technology class. As a group project, she and two teammates needed to build a tower as tall as possible with marshmallows and macaroni pasta. Kiera came up with an idea to glue the base of tower onto a board so the structure would be more stable. One of the teammates liked the idea, but the other one had doubts. "Are we allowed to do that?", asked the boy. Kiera replied, "No one said that it was not allowed." So they did what Kiera suggested. In the end, her team was the only team that glued the base onto a board and won the competition. Other teams all liked the idea. There was just no time for them to do the same after they found out about it and before they had to submit their projects.

I remember how Kiera's eyes sparkled when she told me the story. I could tell that she felt very proud of herself for taking a chance and taking a risk. I feel very proud of her too.

Things could have turned out differently. Kiera's teacher might have said that gluing was not 'allowed' and their project could have received a bad grade. But it doesn't matter. It was worth trying! Trying different things, going about things in different ways, and failing are all parts of learning. It might seem that if we suppress our mind and thoughts, contain ourselves in a box of made-up rules and not step out even one step, then we would not make any 'mistakes'. We would not look bad in front of others. We would be safe and would fit in with others. But the danger of taking such a so-called safe approach is that we may gradually lose our creativity, imagination, and uniqueness until eventually we lose ourselves. We run a huge risk of becoming mediocre and dull.

I am very impressed that you thought of a smart way to make your project unique. You stuck with your idea even when people around you had doubts. I am happy for you that this time the result turned out to be good, Kiera. Of course, the result might have been the opposite. Your teacher might have given you a hard time and punished you for gluing the base onto a board. You would have gotten a taste of what it's like to not be appreciated for being different and creative. But it does not matter. Fear can't and shouldn't control us. We can't let fear stop us from letting our true selves shine.

I love you very much. - Mama

Six

June 7th, 2016

Bamboo, My Favorite Plant in the Whole Wide World

Growing up in Chengdu, China felt almost like growing up in a bamboo forest. Throughout middle school and high school, I had annual weekend field trips to nearby mountains. On the bus rides, once getting outside of the city wall, I would look out of the bus window and look for gray brick-roofed farmhouses nestled in bamboo plants appearing on the horizon, far away at the end of open fields. I enjoyed seeing light smoke from cooking rise from the chimneys and above the top of bamboo branches, and eventually disappear into the gray sky.

In the city, there were lots of bamboo in parks too. The park that had the most bamboo was Wang

Jiang Gong Yuan, the one next door to Sichuan University. I loved going there and collecting bamboo needles. I called these things bamboo needles because they looked thin and sharp like needles. Actually they were soft, baby green colored young bamboo leaves just coming out. I was very good at spotting them and pulling them out. It would take me less than half an hour to collect a big handful of needles. It was fun to me. I liked the fresh smell of bamboo too. Sometimes, it could take me longer to collect a handful because there were very few bamboo needles on low branches that a young kid like myself could reach, then I would have to venture further away from my parents to find them. There was a very short window of time before bamboo needles grew thicker and became more like a part of the plant.

Bamboo can be used in many different ways. Bamboo shoots are one of my favorite foods. I like their tender and fresh taste. Spring is the best season for tasting fresh bamboo shoots as they just come out of the ground. People in my hometown prepare them in various ways, such as stewing, sautéing, making salads mixed with spicy dressing, etc. Sometimes, they can be hard to chew if they are not harvested at the right time.

MY DEAR DAUGHTER

Even with occasional disappointments, I don't remember ever getting tired of having bamboo shoots.

Bamboo plants are widely used in China in construction, furniture, crafts, baskets, and many different household goods. My personal experiences include having a bamboo steamer, bamboo mat for my bed during hot summers, a bamboo chair, bamboo table, bamboo basket, bamboo pencil holder, bamboo chopsticks, etc.

The reason why bamboo can be used in so many different ways is because of its flexibility and strength. How flexible and strong is it? Imagine a person (or a panda) standing on the top of a bamboo branch, and the branch getting pushed down and up, but not breaking. This was pictured perfectly in the movie "Crouching Tiger Hidden Dragon". Flexibility and strength are among the most desired characteristics described in the philosophy in "Tao Te Ching", the book written by Laozi, one of the greatest Chinese philosophers ever. Very few natural things in the world possess both qualities at the same time. Which one would you think would more likely survive in a category 3 hurricane, a tall straight pine tree or a curved palm tree? Obviously, we see more palm trees by the shore. Just like palm trees, bamboo is able to bend its branches when encountering strong forces.

Only a few years ago, I learned about another amazing characteristic of bamboo. It takes at least three years for bamboo plants to take hold in a new environment and grow their root systems. Once that's done, the bamboo shoots start to appear out of ground and grow very fast. How fast? Some bamboo can grow three feet each day! They become unstoppable. This reminds me of 'delayed gratification'. In order to achieve our ultimate dreams and goals and to live a happy and balanced life, we choose to forego today some things like tasty foods, fun activities, instant happiness and gratification. It's like not going to a party or movie, hanging out at Starbucks, or checking out friends' posts. Instead, we choose to spend time and focus energy on sharpening our minds, building healthy bodies, getting to know the world, and adventuring into areas that we are fascinated about. For example, we spend time reading, practicing gymnastics, painting, crafting, working on projects you want to work on, learning about what's new in the world, exploring nature, etc. I am not suggesting that you not have any fun. I am saying that it's better to spend some time on fun things but more time on building up for your future when you are young, creative, and full of energy. There is a limit to how much time that a person can spend working throughout her lifetime. The more you do when you are younger, the less you have to do when you are older and likely feeling less energized.

One last and best reason why I love bamboo is, you guessed it, because of my grand pandas, Pandy, Pauline, Pando, Pawlie, and Pandora!! Thanks to bamboo, they grow and become stronger every day.

I love you very much. - Mama

Seven

June 14th, 2016

Free Hamilton Tickets? YES!

You know more than I do how hard it is to get tickets to Hamilton - the hottest Broadway show ever. I mean it is not only difficult but also costly. The box office price for tickets ranges from $85 to $300, but tickets were selling on StubHub for $772 and above. The cost of tickets has more than doubled to a starting price of $1,592 on June 3rd. Prices zoomed up a day after some news reporter said that Lin-Manuel Miranda was leaving the production on July 9th. The highest asking price found on StubHub for the July 9th show is $9,975 for a second-row seat in the orchestra.

People said that there were many different ways one could possibly get a ticket: winning the ticket lottery; winning the regular lottery; or winning a Nobel prize because Miranda won a Nobel prize for literature, so you could casually bump into him and ask for a ticket.

But really, how do you get to go to a show for free?

Did you realize that YOU already made it happen?! No, you didn't? Then let me explain.

You worked hard to buy three sets of tickets at face value , with two to four tickets in each set. Later when you sold two sets of them, a total of four tickets for a price that was three times your original cost, you not only covered the cost of the tickets you used yourself, but also made some profit. Let's look at some simple math: you purchased eight tickets at $200 per ticket for a total cost of $1600; you sold 4 tickets at $700 per ticket and received $2800. You not only recovered the $1600 spent on all tickets, but also made $1200 in profit and still had four tickets you could use for yourselves. In other words, by taking the action to purchase eight tickets at face value, you in effect won yourself free Hamilton tickets and some extra cash!

Of course, these kinds of good results don't happen automatically. We call them using "Other People's Money (OPM)" or resources to generate returns. It requires: 1) An eye to spot opportunities, in this case an overwhelming demand for Hamilton tickets; 2) Immediate action, in this case staying up after 12am determined to buy tickets right after they went on sale; 3) A willingness to take a calculated risk, in this case that people would no longer want to pay high prices to see Hamilton and that you would then have to sell tickets at discounted prices and lose money.

You see, many people will only think about getting whatever number of tickets they need and be happy about getting them at face value. They would never think about getting extra tickets for the benefits of going to the show for free plus earning some profit. Perhaps this is not their choice. Or they don't really want to put in the effort or to face potential risks. These are differences between you and them.

We knew a man who did something similar, but on a larger scale. Many years ago, he purchased a large piece of land, went through whatever was required to divide the land into four lots, built a house on each of them, sold three and kept one for his family. He was able to cover the land and construction costs with proceeds from selling three houses. In the end, he earned a house for himself for free.

What other opportunities can you think about? Keep your eyes open and brains going so you can spot new opportunities and work on them!

I love you very much. - Mama

Eight

June 15th, 2016

Starbucks Coffee I

Honestly, I did not know what I should do when Kiera came over to me, looking very upset, and expressed her unhappiness about the wrong drink Morgen got her at the Starbucks counter in Barnes & Noble. Should I tell her that I was sorry but you together made a mistake, and it was what it was? Should I give her money and let her get another one? Should I march over to the counter and ask for something different? I was not sure. But I definitely would not blame you for the situation and make you feel even worse. That simply would not help.

You know me. I take all opportunities to let you experience and learn about the world. Then I thought immediately: why not let you practice fixing the situation yourself? I was not sure what the Starbucks worker's reaction would be if you went and asked for an exchange. I was not sure whether the worker would agree to give you a replacement without charging you. I was not sure how your feelings might be hurt if the worker said mean words or gave you a mean look. I just thought if we didn't try, we would never find out. So I decided to convince you to go back to the counter and try.

Initially, you did not want to go back to the counter. It could be because of fear, embarrassment, doubt, or all of these. I myself felt unease too when thinking about asking for another drink without paying. I did not know if they would say yes or think that I was crazy. I knew how unhappy Kiera felt and how much she wanted to get a drink of her liking, but I was not willing to give in and just give her money to buy another one. I felt that if we just walked out of Barnes & Noble without trying, you would not like this memory or even yourself as much whenever you thought about this experience in the future. I almost gave up on persuading you. But I tried one last time after we had purchased books and were ready to leave. This time you decided to go back and try. Kudos to you!

MY DEAR DAUGHTER

Mother hens always want to protect their chicks. I was standing far away but paying close attention to your interaction with the worker. I was ready to walk up and stand by you if the worker gave you a hard time. I am so glad that I did not do that. You were brave and handled the situation well yourself.

What was there to lose, really? You already had the wrong drink in your hand. If you tried, you might change that reality and get what you wanted. If you did not try, you still had the drink you didn't like and nothing was going to change. You chose to put aside your fear, and to do something to change your situation that day. I was very proud of you!

At this point, I am pretty sure that you will always try when encountering situations like this. This was proved when Morgen asked to re-make Kiera's drink order again at the Main Street Starbucks shop. The possible answers you will get are "yes" and "no". If you already have something unwanted in your hands, then you have nothing to lose and only upside potential by trying.

I love you very much. - Mama

Nine

June 18th, 2016

Starbucks Coffee II

I always puzzle how Starbucks Coffee is so popular. An average cup of flavored coffee costs $5 there. That means someone buying coffee there every weekday would spend $25 each week and $100 each month on coffee alone! That's not a small amount of money.

I guess what you get from Starbucks is not just a cup of coffee, but also a feeling of being cool, sophistication, a chic and modern environment, music, and a chance to bump into other seemingly cool people. But going there every day and dropping $5? I still don't get why some people do that.

I appreciate that, a few days ago, my daughters got to practice there and learned the importance of communications, bravery, taking risks....so maybe those cups of drinks were worth every penny. I am not complaining. My mind is telling me though that you could have had similar experiences in other coffee shops or stores.

Let's see what $100 per month can mean in a longer time frame. If you put aside $100 every month and earn 6% interest for 10 years, you will accumulate over $16,700 at the end of the 10-year period. If you do that for 20 years, you will have $46,800, and after 30 years, you will have $100,500. This shows the Time Value of Money and the Magic Power of Compound Interest. If you find a way to earn a higher interest rate, say 8%, you would accumulate $18,700, $59,300, and $146,800 at the end of 10, 20, and 30 years, respectively. The Magic Power of Compound Interest is amazing!!

So please treat any small amounts of money seriously. One penny saved is one penny earned. They can only come from your hard work. They are all your soldiers that work hard and can help you achieve financial independence. The sooner you start keeping your soldiers around, instead of spending them away, the sooner you can achieve financial freedom. Don't let them slip out of your pocket easily.

If you drink your soldiers away for the next twenty years and only then start gathering them, you will only end up with $16,700 thirty years later, instead of the possible $100,500 if you were to start now. You don't need me to explain to see that the difference is huge. That's called the Time Value of Money. Invested money needs time to grow. You need both time and lots of soldiers by your side. As long as you start now gathering your soldiers and building your armies (making money from doing things that you are good at and love doing) and make them work for you (finding ways to earn interest or other income), I promise you will earn your financial independence and freedom to allocate your own time before you reach age 35. That's 21 years from now for Morgen, and 23 years for Kiera.

How do I know that? Because Mama came to this country without any money, so I know what can be achieved in twenty years. I had no specific goals or direction twenty years ago, but I was lucky and able to accumulate something. In comparison, now you already know what to ask from the universe and also know to carry out a plan towards reaching your goals, so just imagine what's possible for your future! Twenty years seems to be a long time, especially when you are so young. It will pass more quickly than you can imagine, though. When you get there and look back in time, I am confident that you will have accomplished what you set out to achieve. You will be very proud of yourself.

One less cup of Starbucks coffee, one less smoothie, one less cup of ice cream, one less shirt that's not needed in order to achieve financial independence in the future.... these are all delayed gratification. It's very tempting to just give in. It takes strong mental muscles to do things that others do not do. But imagine what's ahead of you. I am not saying that you should never get a $5 coffee. On the contrary, you should sometimes splurge on yourself, setting aside some funds so you can occasionally treat yourself for your efforts. 'Occasionally' is the key word here. Splurging too often is not delayed gratification, but instant gratification.

Plus, seriously, no one really thinks those sugary treats are good for their health. Even the feeling of satisfaction that they seem to bring is short-lived.

MY DEAR DAUGHTER

Only things like friends, books and experiences in faraway places will bring long-lasting joy, wisdom, and inner-peace.

I love you very much. - Mama

Ten

August 30th, 2016

Whatever You Do, Give it Your All

Tomorrow, you will have you first-ever paid work. I am very excited for you, Morgen!

I imagine that you must feel excited, nervous, and eager to do a great job, all at the same time. At age 14, I never thought about working or making money for myself. I did not know what working meant until after graduating from college. You are already way ahead of me just because of your courage and desire alone.

People who have achieved extraordinary results, all have something in common. That is to do their very best, no matter what they choose to do. They think a lot about what results they want to achieve, what needs to be done, what can be done better, and how they can achieve the desired results. They pay close attention to goals and details, and work continuously until completion. When they encounter obstacles, they come up with ways to solve problems and then keep going. They never let temporary setbacks cloud their vision and never lose sight of their end goals.

There is no job too small or too big. When we complete a job to our satisfaction, we not only learn to do that job well and get paid, but also acquire skills needed and train our minds to be strong. Somewhere in the future, we will be able to utilize these skills and our strong minds for some bigger tasks. We might not know now when, where or how, but trust me, we will benefit from them. And even if we never get to use them (very unlikely), at least we did our best and will have no regrets!

Do your best tomorrow and have fun! If you are not having fun, the kids you babysit won't have fun either. You had many babysitters before the age of 12. You know what makes a babysitter wonderful. You always wanted someone who were caring and kind, and who could play with you and be your friend. So be that person for the kids whom you babysit.

I am very proud of you!

I love you very much. - Mama

Eleven

October 16th, 2016

Living for a Purpose

People often say that the world is not a fair place.....some people have more and some people have less; some are born rich and some are not. Actually, I would say that there is one thing that is fair, that everything in the world will eventually cease to exist, sooner or later. This may sound pessimistic, but it is really just a natural law. Look around and you will find examples everywhere. A castle crumbles down hundreds of years after it's built; grass turns green in spring and yellow in winter; trees grow tall but eventually fall in 10, 50, or 500 years; lions are considered kings of the animals but will stop running one day; a baby starts her journey towards death the moment that she is born; even the earth will someday cease to exist, and maybe even the universe too.

If no one can escape death, then what's there to be afraid of? We should just make the best of life! Some people are remembered, like Leonardo da Vinci as an inventor and artist, like Anne Frank as a little optimistic storyteller, like Lin-Manuel Miranda as a genius Pulitzer Prize-winning composer. Many others, including kings and wealthy men, came and went, and have left without leaving any mark. You see, what makes life meaningful is not power or money, but one's journey from the beginning to the end and its impact on the world.

What do we come to this world for? There are natural disasters, imperfection, and problems in this world. We come to respond to these, create solutions, make people's lives better and the world a more beautiful place. Imagine if there were only daylight but no night, there would be no dark evenings and less need to invent light bulbs, but there would be a greater need to help people stay cool and fall asleep. Imagine if there were no harsh winters or pouring rain, there would be less need to help people stay warm and dry, and therefore less need to invent the lean-to, house, and apartment building. Human beings are creative and capable. With our creativity, talent and strength, we can do amazing things. It does not take a genius to change the world. Desire and effort will do the job.

Believe it or not, you are already doing your part. Kiera volunteers to read paragraphs with Chinese names in them in class because she wants her teacher and classmates to know how to pronounce and not have to struggle with them. Morgen sources used American Girl dolls, donates cleaned and refurbished ones to little girls that can't afford them, and puts smiles on their faces, brightens their lives, and fills their hearts with hope. Your father comes up with the Samaritags solution to address people's natural forgetfulness and help good Samaritans do good deeds, and Eco Cool to cool hot rooms in houses naturally and economically.

Let's continue to do our part. I am very proud of you.

I love you very much. - Mama

Twelve

October 27th, 2016

Books Are Our Lifelong Friends

Last night, Morgen asked me why reading books is like feeding our souls. I did not immediately have a clear answer. I had not thought about this question thoroughly myself. I am sorry, Morgen.

Now I want to pull my thoughts together and share with you why I think reading is important. In the last ten years, I have read self-help books, personal finance books, and some best-selling business books. These books kept me going with my work and pursuing personal financial goals.

I remember clearly that the first of these books I read was *The Millionaire Next Door*, a personal finance book by Dr. Thomas Stanley. Well, I did not really 'read' it. I listened to the audio book borrowed from the library. We bought a cassette player for $10 for me (instead of other costly modern equipment). It turned out that the $10 cassette player was the best investment ever made, with so little input but such great return. I became very interested in the book and listened to it back and forth, definitely more than twice for some parts. It taught me so much and gave me such impact that I remember seeing my eyes lit up in a mirror like I had just awakened. That was when I returned to work after my maternity leave from giving birth to Kiera. I remember saying to myself that I had two kids and needed to be more responsible. In the short 10 years afterwards, I lived according to this book. It practically became my bible.

I hope that you will choose to read this book someday, although it may or may not have the same impact on you. Where you are today is very different from where I was when I was thirty years old. My parents had never taught me anything that the book revealed; but you might have heard some of the principles from your Dad and me or seen us putting them into action. Whether you end up reading it or not, I believe sooner or later you will find your own "The Millionaire Next Door" book.

After *the Millionaire Next Door*, I read *The Millionaire Mind, The Secret of Millionaire Mind, Rich Dad Poor Dad,* and on and on. Like I said, I read mostly personal finance, self-help, and business books. I went to Borders, a chain bookstore like Barnes & Noble, next to my One Wall Street office during lunch time, when I did not have any client lunch meetings or internal seminars. I finished reading numerous books in that way. I listened to books on tape on the subway and LIRR train rides too. Sometimes I was so tired that I would fall asleep while listening, and I just rewound and continued listening when I woke up.

Besides text books, I did not read much growing up. Back then in China, parents and teachers wanted mostly for children to do well in school. Otherwise they did not encourage or cultivate their interest in reading. I always struggled and had trouble writing essays because I had no inspiration and no idea what to write about. I was always lacking words. Obviously, I read too little. I was a good student with good grades from elementary school to graduate school, but I hardly remember what I learned at college. It's sad and regretful. I feel that I wasted all these years until I was thirty years old and I started to read. I wish that I read all kinds of books when I was little and growing up. Through reading, I could have discovered what life can be, learned from other people's experiences, and figured out what I wanted for my life. Through reading, I could have better understood people, their feelings, their stories, and in turn better understood myself. Through reading, I could have known better how to handle myself, make fewer mistakes, and achieve more than I did. If only I could rewind my life like rewinding the cassette player.

Since I left my job at BNY Mellon, I read some traditional Chinese philosophy books. They really help me calm down, look into myself, and find what I want for my life. I wish I had read them sooner.... my life might have been on a totally different path. But it's never too late, is it?

Now, I read not only self-help, personal finance, business books, but also philosophy, biography, psychology, and education books. I used to think that reading fiction was a waste of time. Actually, good fiction like classic novels are very good tools to learn about human nature, feelings and emotions. There must be something incredible about the classics that makes them last, right?

You can read about whatever interests you, whether it's people, history, philosophy, fantasy, sports, cooking, gardening, science, technology, astronomy, design, architecture, art, etc. I recommend biographies of extraordinary people. These biographies are beneficial because we get to see the world through these extraordinary people's eyes and learn to better the world like they did through their actions.

I thought that there must be lots of articles out there on why people read and how reading benefits people. So I searched the web and found the following six widely referenced and science-backed reasons:

1. To reduce stress
2. To keep the brain sharp and slow down memory loss
3. To stave off Alzheimer's - intellectual activity strengthens the brain against diseases
4. To sleep better - bright lights including those from electronic devices wake up the brain
5. To become more empathetic (fiction is good for this)

6. To ease depression (self-help books can be good for this)

There are so many reasons why people read. Everyone has her own answer. To me, reading helps me find myself, be myself, and feel peace with myself. So why wait, go read a book you like now.

I love you very much. - Mama

Thirteen

November 2nd, 2016

The Schedule of Life

Imagine in a faraway place, a little baby girl is born. She drinks, eats, plays, and grows. She goes to preschool, kindergarten, elementary, middle, and high school. She travels to different places, meets different people, and dreams about what she wants to become when she grows up. She enters into college and studies subjects that she is interested in. She finds jobs and works for forty years. Along the way, she is married to her Mr. Right and has children of her own. All along, she puts away a portion of her income and invests money for the future. Thanks to her hard work, time and the power of compound interest, she has enough money saved up and enjoys her retirement and grandchildren.

This is probably what a person's life is like in the Game of Life. The picture seems right but has some flaws.

Flaw #1: we assumed that she found jobs she liked and got paid well. In reality, some people don't get paid well at all.

Flaw #2: we assumed that she had the discipline to put aside a portion of her income for the future. In the American consumer culture, forget about investments, people just can't save. Numerous surveys show that one out of three people here don't have any savings; two out of three people have less than $1,000 saved regardless of age group or income level.

Flaw #3: we assumed that she understood the time value of money, knew how to handle money and make money grow. Studies show that more than two thirds of people in their 20s and 30s don't have much concept of this topic.

Flaw #4: probably the most important one, we assumed that she was able to work continuously for forty years. In reality, some people can't work for long periods of time due to illness or lack of available jobs, especially later in life.

MY DEAR DAUGHTER

Let's look at the story of Mother Nature. In spring, the weather turns warm, rains wet the earth, and plants grow. In summer, the sun gets hot, bees fly around, and plants blossom. In fall, leaves change color, plants bear fruits, and squirrels gather nuts. In winter, trees lose their leaves, snow falls, and squirrels hibernate. This is nature in its harmonious state. Imagine in a spring with little rain, sprouts would not erupt; in a violently stormy summer, plants would be flooded; in an unexpectedly cold fall, fruits would be destroyed before they could be picked and stored away. If any unexpected natural disasters occurred, there would not be much food harvested for the winter and next year.

What do the life of the little girl in a faraway place and Mother Nature have in common? They both follow the laws of nature. Unexpected events, setbacks, and detours can happen any time and without notice. For Mother Nature, a good year can follow a disastrous one, but we human beings only live once. That's the difference. The good news is that human beings are an amazing species and are given great powers and abilities when created. You can choose to live a life that's different from that in the "Game of Life" if you want to and put in enough effort.

Benjamin Franklin is quoted to have said, "Early to bed and early to rise, makes a man happy, healthy, and wise". The early bird catches the worm. Instead of going through life at an even pace, we can choose to have a front-loaded schedule. By that I mean you build up from early on, put in extra energy and work harder when you are young. That way, you give time and the power of compound interest a chance to work their magic while you continue to work hard. Then there is a good chance you will end up with abundant wealth sooner than those who wait, like that little girl from a faraway place.

You can already guess that the least desired life schedule would be a back-loaded one, which is to take it easy in one's 20s, 30s, 40s, and 50s, and have to work hard in one's senior years. That's like missing the planting in spring, growth in summer, and harvest in fall, and then having to come up with grains and nuts for winter and the next year.

I love you very much. - Mama

Fourteen

November 18th, 2016

Kai Yuan Jie Liu (开源节流), a Personal Wealth Secret

Do you remember the water cup experiment that we did? We poured water in a regular plastic water cup, cut various holes in the cup, and compared speeds at which the cup could be filled based on the amount of water going in and out. What happened was that the more water going in at a faster speed, and the smaller and fewer holes in the cup, the quicker the cup was filled. If the amount of water going in is less than that going out, the cup could never be filled. Imagine water from more than one water hose coming in at high speed, what would happen? How quickly would the cup be filled?!

This is a perfect demonstration of a profound Chinese philosophy - 'Kai Yuan Jie Liu' (开源节流). 'Kai Yuan' means to open up/broaden the source. 'Jie Liu' means to regulate the flow.

In personal finance, this means to generate income from multiple sources and to spend wisely, so that expenses do not exceed income. In nature, this means planting more trees than are cut down so there are always forests. Can you think of any other examples of 'Kai Yuan Jie Liu'?

I shared with you the first-ever personal finance book I read, *The Millionaire Next Door* by Dr. Thomas Stanley. This book taught me tons about how to 'Jie Liu', or how to regulate expenses. It made such an impact it's like it changed how my brain was wired. The only exception is that I talked your father into buying a place to live in rather than renting early on, before I read this book, because I had already believed in owning rather than renting. Paying rent is like helping landlords with their mortgages. In the end, landlords own properties, but tenants don't.

Here are three rules of 'Jie Liu' from the book that benefitted me the most:

MY DEAR DAUGHTER

1. Spend money on things that appreciate, not depreciate. Some things appreciate, meaning their value goes up in time. Other things depreciate, meaning their value goes down in time. Things that appreciate include land, buildings, certain kinds of stocks and bonds, artworks, antiques, and maybe intellectual property. Things that depreciate are almost everything else including cars, clothing, furniture, cell phones, computers, and on and on. The moment a brand-new car is sold and driven out of a dealer's parking lot, it will lose 10% of its original value. Let's say that you paid $50,000 for a new car and needed to sell it immediately for whatever reason. You could only sell it at a discount, so you would probably get back only $45,000 or even less. The car would then keep on losing value over time. Spending a lot of money on cars and other depreciating assets is like kissing your money goodbye.

2. Invest in yourself. The greatest assets a person has are her mind and body. Never begrudge money and time spent to keep your mind and body healthy and fit. If you find a book you like, get it and read it. If you are interested in yoga, sign up for a class. If you like swimming, obtain a membership at a pool and hire a coach. Buy

yourself healthy food and eat balanced meals. We don't need to stuff ourselves, but we should eat enough and eat well.

3. Buy quality clothes with classic styles and materials that will last for years. They will make you look good and feel confident. You will want to wear them again and again. The result is that the cost per wear could actually be much lower than that of lower priced items. Cheap fashionable clothes never last long because you will probably find that you no longer like or want to wear them again after wearing them only a couple of times. It might be tempting to buy ten cheap shirts instead of two nice ones when you are young and just starting out, and money is not abundant. I doubt you would want to wear those ten shirts though in the years ahead. But you might well be wearing those two nice ones again and again. Adding a couple of nice pieces of clothing each year, you will be able to accumulate a wardrobe of clothes that you love in a few years. Now there is another incentive to try to keep your body in shape......that is so that this strategy can work.

I admit that this is not an expert handbook on 'Kai Yuan', meaning broadening the source. I worked, managed investment property, and invested in some stocks and mutual funds. I knew some theories outside of these conventional methods but I did not act upon them. Unfortunately, lack of action means lack of experiences as well as results. I might be a little afraid of change and uncertainty. But the real reason might be that I did not fully realize what I wanted for my life or I did not set appropriate goals. So maybe one day, you will figure out better than I have the secret of Kai Yuan, through trial and error, learning from others, and taking action yourself. I have confidence in you!!

I love you very much. - Mama

Fifteen

November 20th, 2016

Snowballing Your Friends

I was little surprised when I received a WeChat message from a woman who I barely knew. She asked to get together for lunch at a dim sum place. "Sure", I replied. I was curious to find out why she wanted to meet up.

How did we meet each other? You know the story. We met at Carlos Pizza when I went there to pick up our pizza order on a Friday afternoon in April this year. She was trying to place an order for her daughter's birthday party, but she could barely speak English and did not know what to order either. I explained the types and sizes, and helped her figure out how many pizzas to order based on the number of guests. We added each other as a contact on WeChat (a

Chinese social network platform). I thought that was that and maybe we would never see each other again even if we lived in the same small town, because I really did not know who she was, which city she came from, or what she liked.

Two weeks ago, we got together for lunch. She drove to our house to pick me up. The moment I got into her car, she said that she wanted to make friends with me because she enjoyed reading my posts on WeChat very much and thought of me as an interesting person with an open mind, and lots of quality characteristics based on my posts. Just like Instagram and Facebook, people can see each other's posts once they connect with each other on WeChat. I would be able to see her posts and she would be able to see mine. She apologized for not being in touch for months. She explained that she had just given birth to her second child when we first met at Carlos, so needed time to recover and take care of her newborn son.

Basically, she got to know more about me through my posts, thought I was a cool person to be friends with, and took it in her own hands to approach me. I thought a lot about her actions and reasoning, and suddenly realized that this was probably a reason why she ended up living in a large house in Sands Point...even if living in a place like that was not her original goal. She knows what she wants and is not afraid to pursue what's good for her. In contrast, I have rarely approached anyone to say I admire you, I like you, or I want to be your friend. I guess I am too proud and scared of rejection. The result is that I missed a lot of opportunities to build friendships with and learn from people that I admire. No one can conquer the world on her own...

This reminds me of your good friend's mom. She pretty much took the same action. She approached me on a Long Island Rail Road train riding home from work one day. I was having a casual conversation with another passenger next to me about how my dress looked professional and elegant, and how I felt that it was more like my uniform and necessary for my work. She came to me and introduced herself after having heard that conversation. Later on, she invited us to her party where you met your friend for the first time.

The professor whom I was a research assistant for during my graduate school years also took a similar approach. He was a Management professor and attended lots of events. After each event, he would write a thank you letter to the speaker of the event to express his gratitude and admiration. He would also suggest meeting in person and sharing thoughts at the speaker's convenience. Since he had only one arm (the other was lost in an accident many years ago), I typed up these letters for him. In a silent way, he showed me how he grew his circle of friends.

Reading *The Snowball: Warren Buffett and the Business of Life*, a biography of Warren Buffett by Alice Schroeder, I learned that Buffett built wealth like rolling a snowball. He also accumulated friends like rolling a snowball. His principle for building a gigantic snowball was to find the right kind of snow and a long slope, and roll. Once he identified a person as a friend, just like a good investment , he kept his friendship close and never broke their relationship (with one exception when a guy chose not to be in the Buffett circle).

Who are our friends? Friends should inspire each other, learn from each other, help each other, care about each other, and have fun together. It helps to keep you on the right track if your friends also live their lives with purpose, try to be their best, and make the world a better place. Life will be a lot more interesting if we have friends in different fields, with a variety of hobbies. People change, so while snowballing, it's ok to leave people who are no longer inspiring to you and find others who inspire you.

I see wonderful lives ahead of you. I am very excited for you.

I love you very much. - Mama

Sixteen

November 29th, 2016

1,000 Kilometers in 2016 - What I Learned from Running

You might be wondering how I felt when I finally achieved my goal of running 1,000 kilometers in 2016. I wondered myself many times in the past months. Would I feel excited, proud, happy, or very tired when I finished? Or would I feel disappointed, sad, regretful, or ashamed if I didn't? Now I can tell you, I actually felt calm as I hit the 1,000-kilometer mark. When I had accumulated 900 kilometers and had less than 100 kilometers left to finish, I was excited and happy because I knew I should be able to finish if nothing out of the ordinary happened. In the end, the finishing line ribbon you created made me feel happy and loved.

This running thing really fell on me by accident. It was never in any of my plans. I did not start running because I searched hard to find what I was good at, or was interested in doing, or would make me happy and found running. I started running once or twice in late December 2015 because I wanted some intense exercises that could help distract me from issues I was worrying about, take my mind off of crazy thoughts, get rid of the negativity inside of me, reduce stress, and help me sleep better. Then I accidentally signed up for the Under Armor You vs. the Year 1,000 Kilometers in 2016 Challenge on the MapMyRun App. For two self-proclaimed math experts, your Daddy did a quick calculation and thought it involved running for two miles twice each week, and I listened to him without double checking or using any of my own brain power. After logging in 2.1 miles on January 3rd, I suddenly realized that something was not quite right. Two miles twice a week would mean 208 miles for a year, which is far less than 621 miles (the equivalent of 1,000 kilometers). His math was completely wrong this time. I recalculated. In order to complete 1,000 kilometers (or 621 miles) in 365 days/52 weeks/12 months, I needed to run about 1.7mile/2.7kilometers each day. This was a bummer! I was not sure if I wanted to or could do so much given that I never ran much prior to 2016. You know the story of me running 800 meters on my high school track as part of PE class tests. I had to drag myself to the finish line and felt out of breath for at least another ten minutes after. But at the beginning of 2016, I needed to get my mind off of negative thoughts. I needed to reassure myself that I could accomplish things if I set my mind to. I decided to stick to it.

A couple of weeks into the Challenge, my right foot started to hurt after running. I would ICE (ice, compress, elevate) my foot after each run to alleviate the pain. The soreness got worse unfortunately. I had to stop running, hoping that my foot was OK and I would be able to run again. I really did not want to fall behind on my challenge shortly after I had started. Then I read that a good pair of running shoes were important and necessary to support the feet and body during running. You see, I thought that people were just being fancy to run in running shoes when they could wear regular shoes. I never thought carefully about why running shoes were invented. I was too cheap to 'waste' money on a pair of proper shoes when I decided to participate in the Challenge. When my foot stopped bothering me, I bought a pair of Nike running shoes (at the discount store Nordstrom Rack) and tried running in them. My foot did not hurt this time! I was back running again.

Unexpected things happen. There are always obstacles that come our way. We will remove them, go around them, and keep moving towards our goals. Of course, knowledge helps along the way. If I had read about running in general, I would have known to wear something more supportive to begin with. I could have avoided my foot injury from the get-go. But it's OK to make a mistake if we learn valuable lessons from it. If we must know everything before making a move, we will never ever be able to do anything!!

I was able to catch up from the delay caused by my foot injury through running a bit more each time. I kept on running about three miles three or four times each week. At the beginning, I got tired easily and had many two-mile runs. Later, I became used to running and increased the distance gradually to sometimes four miles each time. There were days when I did not feel like running because it was cold, raining, snowing, icy, windy, or I just simply was not in the mood. There were times when I started running and then did not want to complete the full distance as scheduled. But I stuck through.

I mostly enjoyed running on my own while listening to wind, birds, and children playing in the playground; seeing that trees gained their leaves back, grass turned green; meeting children who were interested in running a couple of laps around the park with me. In winter, the field was bare and hard. I remember saying to myself "wouldn't it be nice to have a soft grassy field to run on?". In early summer, the grass grew so quickly, and became very deep. I said to myself "it requires so much more energy to run on deep grass, I would rather have short grass or no grass". Early spring and late fall might be the best times in terms of grass conditions, but these times were so short. Don't get me wrong, I am not complaining. On the contrary, I feel very lucky that I have easy access to such a nice field. To me, grass feels a hundred times softer than pavement, which means my feet and knees won't be worn out as much. What I am trying to say is that when I had a no-grass field, I thought it would be so much better to have a grassy field; when I had a grassy field, I learned that it was not perfect or exactly what I was hoping for. Looking back, I realize that things and situations are never perfect.

There are always pros and cons, advantages and disadvantages, wins and losses, give and take. What I can do is to make the best of what I have.

By June 30th, I had run exactly 500 kilometers.

Then came the summer heat. I was nervous about and afraid of sweating too much. The traditional Chinese medicine theory is that blood and sweat come from the same kind of inner supply of natural strength that a person is born with. I know this might sound unimaginable and a bit crazy. But try to imagine that we are born with only one tank of propane gas and we use a tiny bit of the supply every day when we get up and do things we do. I did not want to deplete my gas supply too much from sweating so much. Whether this theory makes sense or not, I ran less often in June and first half of July. I then stopped running completely from July 15th. August was spent on our family vacation visiting London and Chengdu, China. I ran once in Chengdu but not at all in London. I regret it very much and wish I ran at least once in London.

By August 21st when we were back from summer vacation, I knew I was behind. I was so afraid to look at my mileage count and did not want to face the situation. According to MapMyRun, the app I used to track my progress, I ran total 558 kilometers out of 1,000 as of August 27th. There were 127 days left in the year. In comparison, I should have accumulated total 654 kilometers by August 27th, which was 96 kilometers more than what I had. Did this mean that I failed and had to give up on my goal? I did not want to face a conclusion that I could not complete a simple goal that I set for myself......a goal that required only my input and therefore should be one hundred percent under my control? I did not want to disappoint your Daddy. I did not want to lose face in my WeChat friend circle. But most of all, I did not want to disappoint and set a bad example for the two of you.

I was confused, disappointed, and sad. Since I started running and had my foot injury, a few friends suggested that I read books on how to run. Yes, how to run. That might sound funny, but there is a scientific way to everything. One of the books I ordered was a Chinese translation of *What I Talk About When I Talk About Running* by Haruki Murakami, who is an accomplished author and a 26-time marathoner. I was able to bring the book back from Chengdu when we returned from our summer vacation. It was destiny that I had this book to read during this period of time. The book revealed that even for an accomplished, self-controlled, run-loving person like the author, he still had many days when he did not feel like running because of the weather, a busy schedule, not feeling well, or other reasons; but he managed to continue and did what he needed to do. The book inspired me. Thank you, Mr. Murakami!

I had to ask myself some tough questions. Did I realistically think that I could still complete my goal? What did I need to do? How often did I need to run and how many miles each time? I carefully did the math again. The calculation showed that I needed to run 2.6 miles/4.4kilometers per day every day (or 18 miles per week) for the rest of 2016 in order to finish 1,000 kilometers. Or I could run for more miles each time and less frequently, like six miles each time three times per week. If I ran six miles each time and four times per week, I would eventually get ahead of schedule. I thought running three or four times each week might be more doable if I could handle six-mile runs. Luckily, I had occasionally run six miles during the first few months because I heard from a more seasoned runner that it worked better for him to run six miles three times a week instead of three miles each day. I decided to try that.

I was very lucky. The universe sensed my desire and made my body strong enough to endure six-mile runs. I tried to run four times each week and added miles gradually. On October 9th, I completed total 771 kilometers with 84 days left in the year. That's exactly where I should be up to that date if I had run 2.74 miles a day every day. I finally caught up with the needed schedule. Yay!

As the 1,000-kilometer goal became much closer, I became more confident. I established a goal, set up a plan to get to my goal, experienced injuries and setbacks, had to adjust my plan, put in extra effort, increased my number of runs each week, and finally caught up. I was pretty sure at that point that I could accomplish my goal. I just needed to continue doing what I was doing, and to avoid any falls or injuries. I was excited.

During the rest of the year, running was fun. I enjoyed six-mile runs and did not feel tired at all. At a pace around 9-9.5 minutes per mile, I could carry on a conversation while running and breathe normally. Kiera asked me how many miles I could run without stopping or feeling really tired.

I could not answer. I tried seven miles and eight miles, and I was still feeling fine. Maybe in the near future, I will try running without stopping until I am tired out. Then I will find out how far I can run.

I feel very fortunate that I have time to spend on things I want to do, like running. I am also very lucky that I have the park to myself when it's nice out, and the tennis center track to run on when the weather gets bad. I appreciate what I have very much.

Here is a list of things that the 2016 running challenge brought to me or made clearer.

1. What running helped me most is to gain my confidence back. I know I can accomplish things if I put my mind to it and don't give up.
2. I learn how important Specific Measurable Achievable Time-bound (SMART) goals are. I would have stopped running many times and could never have gotten to 1,000 kilometers, if I did not set a goal at the beginning of the year.
3. I enjoyed the process of completing the goal MUCH MORE than the result.

4. Through experience, I discovered a pathway to accomplishment: setting goals, constructing plans, measuring progress, overcoming obstacles, adjusting plans, staying focused, and achieving goals.
5. Always try something new so that I can find out for myself what I am good at or interested in. Who knew that I could run?
6. It's OK to make mistakes. We learn from them. If we have to know everything before we can make a move, we can never ever move!!
7. Things don't always go the way I want them to. There will always be obstacles and setbacks. It's understandable to feel worried, scared, or concerned when I fall into undesirable situations. Other people's help is important, but I am the only one who is empowered to act and to get myself out of holes.
8. Family and friends are invaluable. They encourage and help me along the way.

I have a healthier mind and body now thanks to running. Join me please. It would be a good warmup for climbing the world's seven peaks...lol

I love you very much. - Mama

Seventeen

December 26th, 2016

Fear is Best Conquered by Ability

What was my biggest fear? You know it….. snakes. I used to have crazy thoughts about being faced by a snake or being wrapped around and suffocated by a snake. They freak me out. Now that I am a mom, I don't worry much about them anymore. What is the chance that a snake would be standing in front of me and I would have to face it alone? Or of a ginormous snake wrapping around me deep in the jungle? Maybe zero except in dreams. Therefore, I no longer consider snakes my biggest fear.

People are afraid of all kinds of things. Heights, darkness, loneliness, monsters, strangers, mice, bugs, rejection, creepy people, water, speaking in public, death, to name a few! Do you know what is said to be Warren Buffett's biggest fear? Losing trust. How about Johnny Depp? He is said to be scared of clowns. Gustave Eiffel, the designer of the Eiffel Tower, was terrified of heights. And yes, irony of ironies, Walt Disney was indeed afraid of mice!!

Even though fears are no small things, don't feel bad if you are afraid of a thing or two, or three. Practically, no one in the world is not fearful of something.

I never liked watching or reading news about struggling individuals and families, family or sexual abuse, or drug-addictions. This type of news was dark and heavy to me. It made me feel very uncomfortable and unsafe. Looking inside, I realized that I was afraid of falling in those situations myself starting out in a totally foreign and new country. I came here without much awareness of these complicated situations. The older I grew, the more I experienced, and the healthier I became economically, the less likely, I realized, it was that I would be stuck in those undesirable situations, and the less I felt afraid. You see, as I achieved more career goals and took on more responsibilities (from Assistant

Treasurer to Managing Director), I earned higher salaries and built up more wealth. Most of all, I became more confident about myself and my ability. When you know what you want and work towards getting it, the likelihood of undesirable things or situations affecting you is reduced.

Here is a secret about me...... I am afraid of water. The thought of not being able to stand up and keep my head above water makes me nervous. I am scared that water would gush into my nose and mouth and I wouldn't be able to breathe. Once I took a swimming lesson and the coach said to me that I was a sinker. What did that mean? I guess it meant that I had the tendency to go down no matter how much I tried to stay afloat. Thanks a lot, coach. Nevertheless, I learned how to swim the backstroke and stay afloat, not facing forward, but facing upward. It's not the most desirable, but at least it will save me from drowning. I would love to be able to swim freestyle. That's one of my goals.

Fear is not something that goes away easily. Sometimes we live with our fears throughout our lives. The more we get to know about ourselves and the world around us, the more things we learn to do, the more likely we fear less. Being brave is not having no fear. Being brave is knowing and accepting our fears and doing everything that we can to become more capable of handling the situations, things, and people that make us afraid.

I love you very much. - Mama

Eighteen

December 29th, 2016

First Things First

How do you spend your twenty four hours each day? Wouldn't it be nice to do everything you love doing? As a student, you sleep for eight hours, go to school for eight hours, and relax and do other things that you feel like doing for the rest of time. As an adult, instead of going to school, you might spend more than eight hours each day working. No matter what you do, how you spend your waking hours makes up who you are. You are what you do.

We are faced with different situations and things every day. Not all things are equal. I like the Eisenhower Matrix time management scheme, which groups all things into four categories: important and urgent, important and not urgent, unimportant and urgent, unimportant and not urgent. The well-known saying goes like this, "what is important is seldom urgent and what is urgent is seldom important." It is very true, if you think about it. And I would add that what is important seldom brings immediate results.

Often, people are so busy dealing with urgent things day after day, month after month. Because urgent things seem to require our immediate attention, we push aside and forget about important things. Months, even years, go by. We suddenly realize one day that we have not done the most important things in our lives.

What is considered important and urgent to one person may not be to others. To me, exercise is very important. It helps me stay fit physically and mentally. Even though routine exercise is crucial for staying in shape, people find different reasons not to exercise: no time, too tired, too much work, etc. They don't consider it urgent until their body sends out signals or breaks down. Some other important but not urgent things include reading, self-reflection, meditation, and planning for the future. None of these things will make a person happier, healthier, or wiser in a day or two. But time will tell. You will see a difference in five, ten, or twenty years.

The most obvious unimportant and not urgent thing, in my opinion, is to check out posts and updates on WeChat, YouTube, and other social media platforms. They are such time killers. You may think that you are getting on for a few idle minutes, but you end up losing half an hour without even noticing.

How do we make sure that we actually end up doing important but not urgent things if they are not pressing and constantly demanding our attention? Put them on a calendar and allocate time for them! You may not have control over everything in life, but at least you have control of how you spend your time. Go for a walk or run at six o'clock if you need to get ready for school or work at seven o'clock in the morning. Stop everything at eleven o'clock and read for half an hour if you go to sleep at eleven thirty in the evening. The secret is to fill your calendar with important things first. Do this for a while, and you will discover that you actually have time for everything. When you take care of important things, you will run into fewer emergencies and headaches. Life can be busy but smooth. Things can fall into place.

One of the things that is worthwhile doing is to spend some time alone by yourself each day, without interruptions from anyone or any electronic devices. Looking inside of yourself, getting to know who you are and what you want your life to be, can help you stay calm and focused. It does not have to be long. Ten or fifteen minutes may be enough. You will probably find this makes a big, almost magical difference.

Besides improving yourself, there are other important but not urgent things like spending time with family and friends, traveling to faraway places, contributing to society, and making the world a better place. Hopefully, your work is your passion. You will be among the lucky few who spend many of their waking hours taking care of important things in their lives.

It is unlikely that your family will walk away from you if you do not stay in touch for a long while. But they are the people that love and care about you the most in the whole wide world. Cherish them when you can. Don't take anyone or anything good for granted. Regrets can't bring people or love back when you no longer have them.

Life is supposed to be a colorful journey with joy, sadness, excitement, setbacks, ups and downs. Stay true to who you are. Do what you are good at and love doing. Meet people that you want to meet. Visit places that you have never been to. Bring positive changes to people around you and the world. Spend your time wisely and you will get to enjoy everything life has to offer.

I love you very much. - Mama

Nineteen

January 17th, 2017

The World Was Wide Enough

You know the lyrics better than I do: "The world was wide enough for both Hamilton and me..."

I wanted to write to you when we first saw the Broadway show *Hamilton* and became familiar with the song, but I procrastinated. Last weekend, we won the theatre lottery and got to sit in front row seats watching history unfolding in musical form right in front of our eyes. It was exhilarating! Then Burr's singing "The world was wide enough for both Hamilton and me" entered my ears. I felt a strong desire to share my thoughts with you. This time, I told myself that I was going to do it right away.

The first time I heard something similar to these words was 16 years ago. I was just starting out in the financial service industry after having graduated from my MBA program. My fellow young coworkers all wanted to get ahead and be promoted. A colleague said to me that the world was big enough for everyone and there was enough to go around. She felt that the competition between her and another co-worker became ruthless and it did not have to be that way. At that moment I was not sure if I believed what she said, because we were all trying to be promoted first and become the boss's favorite. But for some reason, even with my not-so-good memory, I remembered those words. She was from an Irish family that owned a hotel business back in Ireland. It seemed to me that she had figured things out. Later on, she moved on to another department and then another, and became a Managing Director before I did.

By now, I firmly believe that the world is wide enough for everyone who knows what they want. Like what's conveyed in Rhonda Byrne's show *The Secret*, we live in an abundant universe. Most people want money, fame, power, legacy, health, happiness, etc. What everyone wants can be different, however. Even if you want the same thing as the person next to you, there are different ways to get there. Washington, Adams, Jefferson, and Madison all wanted to become the President of United States of America. And they all did, sooner or later, one after another.

An old Chinese saying goes like this "三百六十行行行出状元", which means there are 360 trades and professions and there are geniuses in every trade and profession. Find your passions and interests, use your talents, take actions, and what you want will become a reality.

It's way more effective to spend time on achieving goals and becoming your better self than to spend time on worrying about rivalries and competition. I am not suggesting that we should shield our ears and eyes to what's going on in the world and what others are doing. On the contrary, we should be aware of the latest and greatest happenings in our specific fields and what other major players are up to but still focus more energy on improving ourselves and achieving our goals. Ultimately, it is the best service, product, quality, and character that win people's hearts. Stay positive.

APRIL ZHOU

I am proud of you.

I love you very much. - Mama

Twenty

January 20th, 2017

Pay it Forward

The other day, I found myself in a jam. I needed to find a Chinese landscaping company quickly. Since I never used one and there were not that many Chinese service companies here, I was not sure where to go. Dayidie recently moved into a house with a jungle-like yard. With his limited English, he naturally wanted to hire a Chinese company that he could easily communicate with. I felt that I had to help him as he was new to this country.

In desperation, I sent a message to the local Chinese social media platform WeChat group and asked for help. Five minutes later, someone in the group recommended a Chinese landscaping company and gave me its contact info. I felt relieved.

Thirty minutes later, someone else in the WeChat group asked about the evening parking rules in the Long Island Rail Road parking lot. It had been a while since I last looked at the signs in those parking lots. I remembered a sign saying no parking between 2-5am. Even though I was not a hundred percent sure about the rule, I wanted to pay back the favor. So I wrote "2-5am no-parking rule in the past" and mentioned about signs in the parking lots for verification. And then someone else jumped in to say it's now no parking between 3-5am.

The chain of events reminded me of the term "Pay it forward". Pay it forward is a third-party beneficial concept that involves doing something good for someone in response to a good deed done on your behalf. When you pay it forward, you don't necessarily repay the person who did something nice for you. Instead, you do something nice for someone else.

The concept has a long history. Benjamin Franklin described in his letter to Benjamin Webb in 1784 his intention to help Webb by lending him some money. He did not want to be repaid directly. Instead, he hoped that Webb would at some point meet an honest man in need of financial help and pass the money along to that person.

I first heard about the term when we were at Kiera's annual gymnastics team dinner. At the end of the evening, I found myself standing in front of valet parking with only $20 bills in my wallet. As I was searching my bag for some loose change to tip the valet parking guy, a mom waiting next to us kindly offered $2. I thanked her and asked for her daughter's name so Kiera could bring her money back. But all she said was "just pay it forward". Even though I had done something for others and others for me too in the past, this was the first time that someone said these words to me.

You are both helpful, generous, and kind. I know that you have done many good deeds for others. One never knows when she might need a hand but it will always feel good when she's offered one. Pay it forward.

I love you very much. - Mama

Twenty-One

January 28th, 2017

A Woman That You Grow Up to Become

Have you ever asked yourself who you want to grow up to be? There were and are extraordinary women out there, athletes, entrepreneurs, scientists, investors, artists, performers, creative designers, engineers, astronauts ...... Do you want to be just like any of them? Unfortunately, there is not a manual or a text book that tells us what kind of woman we should become or how to get there. Fortunately, you are more than capable of figuring out how to become your best self that inspires others.

A woman is, first of all, a person. There are a few basic facts about a person. A person comes to this world with nothing, and sooner or later, leaves with nothing as well. Life is short. In between coming and going, it's up to each individual how to show her appreciation for the opportunity to be around in this world.

A person is created with mental and physical abilities to grow, change, and create, just like an infant learns to lift her head, roll, crawl, walk, and run. A person possesses passion and love and is bound to experience ups and downs. The path of pursuing passion, overcoming challenges, and benefiting as many people as possible along the way will ultimately lead one to a fulfilled and happy life.

Passion is something that, once discovered and cultivated, can last through one's life. When I read that the New York Times East Africa Chief Correspondent's passion was simply living and working in East Africa, I was totally surprised. I had doubts initially if it could be called a passion, because I always thought somehow a person's passion needed to be grander or more vocational. As I read on more about how he first wanted to live in East Africa, worked for years in the US to move up in journalism, finally made his way to East Africa and found a way to make a living there, and used his knowledge and experience to correspond Africa stories daily, I realized that it was his true passion. Like Warren Buffett with his investing, people with passion are eager to get up every morning to do whatever is required day after month after year. They just love what they do.

A myth about passion is that it might not be there at this moment, and it's suddenly there at the next. But that is probably far from the truth. People try different things and explore their interests. With effort, practice, and increased skills, interests can develop into passions.

Besides following their passions, there are other things people love. On a small scale, there is love for oneself and one's family. On a big scale, there is love for other people, nature, and the world. Loving oneself means eating nutritious foods, exercising for health and strength, sharpening and broadening the mind, and believing in oneself. Loving the world means appreciating its wonder and diversity, giving back and contributing to a better world. If what you are passionate about doing also benefits other people, then your passion can bring even more joy and be a source of lifetime happiness.

A woman is not a man. Women and men are created differently, with their unique physical and mental strength. Try asking a man to be pregnant with a baby. It can't happen. But he can probably lift up heavy packages much more easily than a woman can. Except for tasks like carrying a baby to maturity, men and women can both do almost everything else. It's just that their approaches on how to do things may differ due to their mental and physical differences. There is no reason for women to always compare themselves with men in everything they do. Instead, sticking to what works for each of us is the way to go.

My mother was born in war-time China in 1940. She lost her father when she and her brother were three and one respectively. My grandmother had to move back in with her maternal family. Growing up poor and being discriminated against, my mother knew from early on that she had to work hard to find a way out. And she did. She went to the best medical school in southwest China and became a doctor. She inspired and encouraged me to be independent and self-sufficient, and to always try to become my better self.

MY DEAR DAUGHTER

When a woman is being her better self, she will more likely meet a loving and inspiring life partner that suits her the best. The law of attraction states that like attracts like. This means that people who love life and have similar values attract each other. It makes sense. Wouldn't it be wonderful if your already interesting life was enriched by a partner and a family? With continuous efforts and open communications between both partners, your life together will be full of joy and happiness.

Throughout life, there will be lots of bumps and obstacles. No one has to do it alone. Instead, ask for a helping hand. It can be a role model from whom you can learn to develop a specific characteristic, like Amelia Earhart's adventurous spirit, Mother Teresa's selfless love, or Aly Raisman's grit and leadership. It can be a mentor that provides advice and advocates for you. It can be a friend that cheers you on. And it can be your family member that brings you a glass of water when you are not feeling well.

How boring would the world be if everyone were the same? Mother Nature certainly does not prefer that. There aren't two things or persons exactly alike. And diversity makes the world colorful and interesting. So be proud of who you are. And grow up to become a woman that you feel right to be.

I am very proud of you. - Mama

Twenty-Two

November 9th, 2017

My Desire to Share "My Dear Daughter" Entries

As you know by now, it is not easy going through tremendous physical, intellectual, and emotional changes all in a span of ten or so years during the adolescent period of life. So far, you both seem to be handling these changes relatively well in the comfort of your own home. But not everyone is so lucky.

There are Chinese students studying in the US away from their families. They struggle to keep up with their academic pursuits while adjusting to the English language and American culture along with coping with their own physical and mental growth all at the same time. I understand how hard it must be because of my own experience while getting my Master of Business Administration degree after coming to the US at a much older age.

There are local students from families that are dysfunctional or lack open communication. These young people can get confused and conflicted, and they often don't feel that they have a safe place to share their thoughts and ask questions.

The first time I watched the 2017 Tony Award winning Broadway show, "Dear Evan Hansen", I was deeply touched by the story. It is about a lonely high school senior suffering from social anxiety who gained a sense of purpose and became socially popular due to a misunderstanding, but eventually had to face deeper and more complex issues. Half of the audience began crying and making loud sounds when pulling out tissues and blowing their noses at some points during the second act. Hearing this, I finally could not stop my own tears from coming out. Later on, I thought about why everyone was so moved. Was it because we felt sorry for Evan Hansen and other characters in the show? I thought that it was also because a lot of people could relate to, to some extent, the emotions and feelings displayed by the characters such as loneliness, helplessness, and yearning for understanding, friendship, and love.

The lyrics from one of my favorite songs in the show, "You Will Be Found", sums it up well:

"Have you ever felt like nobody was there?
Have you ever felt forgotten in the middle of nowhere?
Have you ever felt like you could disappear?
Like you could fall, and no one would hear?
Well, let that lonely feeling wash away
Maybe there's a reason to believe you'll be okay
'Cause when you don't feel strong enough to stand
You can reach, reach out your hand
And oh, someone will come running
And I know, they'll take you home
Even when the dark comes crashing through
When you need a friend to carry you
And when you're broken on the ground
You will be found"

Even though we have our share of disagreements, we are lucky to be able to communicate and support each other most of the time. But there are lots of young people out there, like Evan Hansen and Connor Murphy in the show, who strive for independence without sufficient family and friends' understanding and support. Being alone can be scary, confusing, frustrating, disappointing, and devastating. Then there are some parents, like those in the show, who are equally worried, frustrated, confused, and feeling out of touch with their children. How they wish that their relationships with their children could somehow be different. How they wish that there were a map showing them through uncharted territories. Why don't I share these My Dear Daughter entries? It's worth it even if only one person finds just one of these sentences helpful. It's nice to have a helping hand when it's needed.

I have so much confidence in you.

I love you very much. - Mama

About the Author

APRIL ZHOU is a mother, runner, entrepreneur, and advocate for young people. Raised in China, educated in the US and China, and having worked in multiple industries, she is enthusiastic about helping young people to become confident, independent, and balanced individuals. She lives with her husband and daughters in New York.

www.ingramcontent.com/pod-product-compliance
Lightning Source LLC
Chambersburg PA
CBHW070617050426
42450CB00011B/3075